LEBANON

LEBANON

Mary Jane Cahill

CHELSEA HOUSE

COVER: Baalbek, originally called Heliopolis,
is a city filled with ancient Roman ruins.

3   5   7   9   8   6   4   2

Library of Congress Cataloging-in-Publication Data

Cahill, Mary Jane.
   Lebanon.
   Includes index.
   Summary: Surveys the history, topography, people,
and culture of Lebanon, with an emphasis on the
current economy, industry, and place in the political
world.

1.   Lebanon.   [1. Lebanon]
I.   Title.
DS80.C34   1987   956.92   86-21596

ISBN 1-55546-161-1

Project Editor: Elizabeth L. Mauro
Associate Editor: Rafaela Ellis
Chief Copy Editor: Melissa R. Padovani
Art Director: Maureen McCafferty
Series Designer: Anita Noble
Project Coordinator: Kathleen P. Luczak

ACKNOWLEDGMENTS

The author and publishers are grateful to the following for information and
photographs: Georgetown Design Group, for five photographs by Mokhless Al-Hariri;
Lebanese Information & Research Center; Library of Congress; National Zoological
Park, Smithsonian Institution. Picture research: Imagefinders, Inc. Cover: The National
Council of Tourism in Lebanon.

Contents

Map 6

The Heart of the Mideast 8

Mountain High, Valley Low 17

Lords of the Sea 26

A Conquered People 35

War Without End 48

The People of Lebanon 54

Beirut: City Under Siege 64

Government and Economy 69

Education, Communication, Transportation 76

Five Thousand Years of Culture 81

Ancient Land in a Modern World 86

Index 89

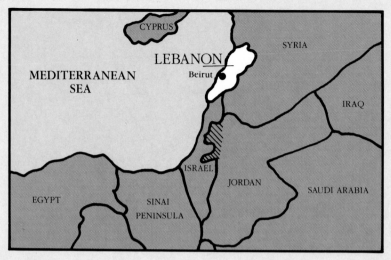

MEDITERRANEAN SEA

Juniya

Beirut

B'abda

Sidon

Jazzin

Hasbani R.

Tyre

Hasbayya

ISRAEL

CYPRUS

LEBANON
Beirut

MEDITERRANEAN
SEA

SYRIA

IRAQ

ISRAEL

JORDAN

SAUDI ARABIA

EGYPT

SINAI
PENINSULA

The Heart of the Mideast

The Biblical land of Lebanon lies at the crossroads of the Middle East, bounded on the north and east by Syria and on the south by Israel. Lebanon's western border is the Mediterranean Sea. The Lebanese are a Semitic people, which means that they speak one of a group of languages spoken in northern Africa and southwest-

The Lebanon Mountains loom over the tiny village of Hasroun

ern Asia. One of these Semitic languages is Arabic, which all Lebanese speak.

Lebanon is a tiny, narrow country, smaller than the state of Connecticut. It is approximately 130 miles (210 kilometers) long and 20 to 60 miles (30 to 100 kilometers) wide, with a total area of only 4,000 square miles (10,350 square kilometers). With a population of about 2.5 million people, it is one of the most densely populated countries in the Mideast.

Before its bloody civil war began in 1975, tourists came from all over the Middle East to sunbathe on Lebanon's snow-white beaches and enjoy its restaurants and hotels. In those days, the world appreciated Lebanon for its sophistication, its tolerance, and

Ruins of an ancient pagan temple in Byblos, one of the oldest cities in the Middle East

its rich, diverse culture. Now the name Lebanon brings to mind car bombings, kidnappings, and round-the-clock warfare.

Long before its daily violence became part of the nightly television newscast, Lebanon played an important part in history and legend. Jesus walked in its southern hills. According to mythology, the goddess Venus met Adonis near Lebanon's coastal plain, and St. George—the patron saint of England—slew his dragon there.

Some Lebanese insist that when the whale cast up Jonah, as described in the Old Testament, he did so on a beach just 20 miles (32 kilometers) south of Beirut, Lebanon's capital city.

Lebanon has been making history since the third millennium B.C., when a tribe of people called the Phoenicians sailed out from the coastal ports of Sidon, Tyre, Byblos, and Beirut. Sailing in the most advanced ships of their day, they traded wares and shared

Ancient inscriptions are carved into rock near the Dog River

the fruits of their civilization with the rest of the Mediterranean world. The Phoenicians were merchants, adventurers, colonizers, explorers, and teachers. Everywhere they went, they spread their wisdom and knowledge. They improved the Egyptian alphabet and taught it to the Greeks and Romans. They showed the Israelites how to build temples and the Romans how to wage war at sea. For a thousand years, until they finally gave way to the more warlike powers who surrounded them, the Phoenicians dazzled the world with their courage and brilliance.

Lebanon has been occupied by Egyptians, Hittites, Canaanites, Greeks, Romans, and Arabs. In the 19th century alone, it was conquered by the Byzantines, the Ottoman Turks, the Mamelukes, and the French. Many of Lebanon's current troubles are rooted in this history of invasion and repression.

Today, Lebanon is an Arab republic. Although its people are heirs to many civilizations, they have a strong Arab identity. Nevertheless, Lebanon is unique among Muslim countries because it has a large Christian population. Some 40 percent of Lebanese are either Maronite Catholic, Greek Orthodox, Armenian Catholic, or members of one of seven other Christian sects. And although they are fewer in number than the Muslims, Christians have dominated Lebanon politically since the country won its independence from France in 1943.

This Christian political power—deeply resented by the Muslim majority—is one of the primary reasons for Lebanon's ongoing civil war. Another reason is that more than 500,000 Palestinian refugees, who lost their homes after Palestine was partitioned in 1948, crowd the shabby tent cities of southern Lebanon and tax a country already overburdened by political and religious differences.

Despite the war, the Lebanese government continues to function. It provides medical coverage for most of its citizens, runs public schools and universities, provides work for the largest percentage of skilled labor in the Middle East, and holds elections whenever breaks in the fighting make these possible.

Because it has for centuries been the banking and commerce center of the Middle East, Lebanon is culturally different from its Arab neighbors. As a result of greater exposure to western society, Lebanon has developed a distinct way of life and some special characteristics that separate it from the more religiously strict Muslim countries of the Mideast. It has a tradition of open-mindedness and tolerance for religious and political dissidents and is a haven for artists, writers, and performers from around the world. For years Beirut was called "the Paris of the East" because it was cul-

13

tured and worldly. Vacationers flocked to its beaches and night-clubs, and shoppers found the latest European fashions in its expensive stores. But now visitors go elsewhere. Violence has turned the hotels into rubble and the beaches into a war zone. Tourism, an important part of the Lebanese economy, has dropped 80 percent since the war began in 1975.

Lebanon is not rich in natural resources. But although the soil is poor, many Lebanese still earn their living as farmers, using irrigation and conservation methods developed since the end of World War II. Lebanon's economy continues to thrive even in the midst of bloody violence. The country has more banks today than

Before the civil war, Beirut was called the "Paris of the East"

Some sections of East Beirut remain prosperous despite the war

when the war began. Still, there is a wide gulf between rich and poor, and not all Lebanese share in their land's prosperity: Rolls Royces and peasant-driven donkeys fight for traveling space in the streets of busy downtown Beirut.

Nevertheless, Lebanon—with the exception of the oil rich Persian Gulf states—still has one of the highest standards of living in the Middle East. Lebanon also boasts one of the highest literacy rates in the region: 86 percent of Lebanese can read and write.

Ancient and modern, rich and poor, razed by mortar fire and then raised anew, Lebanon continues to link East and West, old and new, just as it has since the Phoenicians first sailed from its ports 5,000 years ago.

15

Through a program named the "Green Plan," the government is working to reforest Lebanon's mountains, once lush with cedar and cypress

Mountain High, Valley Low

Lebanon is a rugged, mountainous country unlike any other in the Middle East. It has no great sun-baked deserts, no herds of camels or long lines of palm trees. Lebanon's valleys are green and fertile, and heavy mists obscure its snowy mountain peaks. Its geography is extremely striking and varied, and the sandy beaches of the Lebanese coast are only a 20 minute car ride from the snow-covered slopes of the mountain regions.

The country contains four distinct geographic regions: the coastal plain, the Lebanon Mountains, the Anti-Lebanon and Hermon Mountains, and the Bekaa Valley. The smallest of these regions is the coastal plain, which is no more than four miles (six kilometers) wide and runs along the Mediterranean Sea. Most of Lebanon's major population centers are situated in this narrow strip along the shore.

The low-lying coastal plain is bounded on the east by the rocky spurs of the Lebanon Mountains, the country's most striking physical feature. In fact, Lebanon takes its name from this large mountain range, approximately 100 miles (160 kilometers) long and from 6 to 35 miles (10 to 55 kilometers) wide. Its highest peak, Qurnet as-Sawda, reaches an elevation of 10,131 feet (3,088

The symbol of Lebanon, the cedar appears on the nation's flag

meters) and is located in the center of the country, southeast of the coastal city of Tripoli. The world-famous Lebanese cedar trees grow in the shade of the rugged, snow-capped peak, although few of the towering trees once coveted by the ancient Egyptians for shipbuilding remain today.

Steep gorges cut through the Lebanon Mountains, making them extremely difficult to cross. After reaching its highest elevation, the range slopes southward toward its second-highest peak, Jebal Sunnin, which measures 8,622 feet (2,586 meters). As the mountains continue southward, they gradually become the hills of Galilee, where Jesus and his followers walked. To the east, near

Syria, the range ends in a sheer cliff that drops as much as 3,000 feet (900 meters) in some places.

Farming is difficult in the high mountain regions because the topsoil has a heavy concentration of limestone. At lower elevations, however, the soil is much richer. In the foothills of the Lebanon Mountains, farmers have been terracing their hillsides in exactly the same way since Biblical times. From a distance, these terraced fields look like colorful patchwork quilts laid out in a circular pattern.

The Anti-Lebanon and Hermon Mountains, near Lebanon's eastern boundary with Syria, make up the third geographic region. Although usually thought of as one range, these mountains

Miles of highway have been carved into Lebanon's mountainsides

actually form two ranges separated by the Barada River. Made primarily of limestone, most of these mountains are lower and less rugged than those in the Lebanon Mountain range. They begin with a high peak in the north and slope gently south until they reach dazzling, snow-covered Mount Hermon, 9,232 feet (2,769 meters) above sea level.

The Fertile Bekaa

The fourth great physical characteristic of Lebanon is the Bekaa Valley. Located between the Lebanon Mountains on the west and the Anti-Lebanon Mountains on the east, the Bekaa is part of a chain of valleys and crevasses called the Great East African Rift System that runs southward from the Middle East through Africa to Mozambique. The Bekaa is approximately 110 miles (180 kilometers) long and from 6 to 16 miles (10 to 26 kilometers) wide. The valley's floor, rich with soil and clay deposits washing down from the mountains that surround it, contains some of the most fertile farmland in the Middle East.

The Bekaa Valley is also the largest stretch of level land in Lebanon, reaching its highest point of 3,000 feet (900 meters) at Baalbek, between the Orontes River of the north and the Litani River of the south. At its southern end, the Bekaa becomes hilly, merging with the foothills of Mount Hermon to form the Upper Jordan Valley.

Because there is little rainfall in Lebanon, farmers have had to develop methods of irrigating the Bekaa. Since World War II, productivity in the area has increased dramatically as a result of modern irrigation methods. Even before technology improved farming techniques, though, the Bekaa supplied wheat for much of the world. The Roman conquerors of long ago exported grain grown in this green valley to their imperial capital in Italy, and every invader since has planted the Bekaa's fields and tasted its sweet crops.

Each spring, thousands of Bedouins—the hardy nomads of the Arab world—come to the Bekaa to graze their 60,000 to 70,000 goats and sheep. Most of these Bedouins walk to Lebanon from the Syrian Desert. The trip takes seven days, and the Bedouins walk at night to avoid the scorching sun. When they arrive in the Bekaa, they pitch their black, goat-hair tents on the fringes of cultivated fields and graze their livestock until it is time to move on to the cooler coastal plain. When fall arrives, the Bedouins make their way through mountain passes and return to Syria for the colder months.

Almost any crop can be grown in the Bekaa, but some Lebanese farmers have for centuries cultivated an illegal one: *hashish*, a narcotic substance produced by the hemp plant. The government has tried to force farmers to grow sunflowers instead and has even taken the harsh step of spraying the hashish with chemicals to destroy it. Many Bekaa farmers remain undaunted, however, and continue to raise the outlawed substance.

A Temperate Climate

Lebanon has a typically Mediterranean climate: short, warm winters and long, hot summers. In January and February, the tempera-

New farming techniques have made the Bekaa Valley more productive

ture drops to only 55 degrees Fahrenheit (13 degrees Centigrade), while in July and August it climbs to 90 degrees Fahrenheit (32 degrees Centigrade). Temperatures in the Bekaa Valley are noticeably cooler than those of the coastal plain.

Nearly all of Lebanon's rainfall occurs in the winter months of December through March, when storms that gather in the Mediterranean swirl inland, drenching Lebanon's mountains and valleys. The exposed coastal area receives 30 to 45 inches (75 to 115 centimeters) of rainfall each year, and the mountain regions receive up to 50 inches (125 centimeters). The Bekaa, lying in the shelter of the Lebanon and Anti-Lebanon Mountains, receives much less rain and is almost wholly dependent on drainage or melting snow from the hills. The Anti-Lebanon and Hermon

At one time, snow skiers flocked to Lebanon's mountains

Isolated villages in the northern mountains have for centuries been a refuge for people fleeing religious persecution

The exotic flamingo lives along the Mediterranean coast

The Jeita Grotto, north of Beirut, was discovered in 1958

ranges receive even less rainfall than the Lebanon Mountains. In total, the country has just 70 to 85 rainy days per year, although the precipitation on those days is quite heavy.

Lebanon was once a land of forests, but 5,000 years of logging have wiped out the tall trees. The land has been deforested, plowed, grazed, and burned so often that the soil finally wore out and cannot be regenerated. In place of the noble cedar, Lebanon now produces brush and low-growing trees such as oak, pine, cypress, fir, juniper, and carob.

The loss of the dense forests also meant the end of a wide variety of animals, although bears are still sighted in the Lebanon Mountains. Small animals—deer, martens (furry weasel-like creatures), hedgehogs, squirrels, and hares—are plentiful. Along the coast, marshes attract a variety of exotic birds: flamingos, ducks, pelicans, herons, and snipes. Buzzards, eagles, falcons, and hawks nest in the mountain heights. Migratory birds from Europe and Africa pay yearly visits to Lebanon, and owls, kingfishers, cuckoos, and woodpeckers abound.

Although Lebanon has many rivers, most of them are actually winter streams—made of melted snow from the western slopes of the Lebanon Mountains—that exist only during the rainy season. Three large rivers flow year-round. The Litani River is more than 90 miles (144 kilometers) long and has its headwaters near the ancient Roman ruins of Baalbek. It irrigates the Bekaa Valley and then runs south to the Mediterranean. The Orontes (or *Nahr al-Asi* in Arabic), starts in the Bekaa and flows north to Syria. The Kabir forms the northern boundary between Lebanon and Syria.

Lords of the Sea

Many Lebanese do not think of themselves as Arabs or Christians or Muslims, or even as Lebanese. They consider themselves Phoenicians, descendants of an amazing civilization that came to an end 2,000 years ago.

Man first settled the Mediterranean coast of Lebanon in the Stone Age, around 5000 B.C. These early men were farmers and fishermen, just as many Lebanese are today. In the Bronze Age, around 3200 B.C., another tribe of people—now called Semites because of the language they spoke—settled on the Lebanese coast. This band of newcomers produced exceptional tools and weapons. They began to log the dense cedar forests that covered the Lebanon Mountains and discovered that their timber was in great demand in surrounding territories. None of the important cities of the day in Egypt and Mesopotamia had lumber nearly as useful for shipbuilding as the cedars of Lebanon.

These Semitic people—dark-skinned and wearing clothes dyed a deep purplish red—settled in the port towns of Sidon, Tyre, Beirut, and Byblos. By 3000 B.C., ships from Byblos were hauling their cedar-tree lumber cargo along the seacoast to Egypt and returning to their home port with hatches full of Egyptian

Ancient Semites trekked through the Kadisha Valley to log cedar and cypress from the thickly forested slopes of the surrounding Lebanon mountains

27

Phoenician shipbuilding was the most advanced of its day

gold. The early Lebanese grew even more enterprising: they sent marine fleets to the East and welcomed back cargoes of copper, grain, jewels, hides, and spices from Arabia and Asia.

Soon, neighboring tribal kingdoms began to envy the riches of the four ports, now powerful city-states. The Amorites, the Hyksos, and the relentless Hittites—powerful tribes of the Middle East—each took their turn burning and looting Lebanon's ports. Despite these setbacks, however, the early Lebanese continued to thrive.

Then, around 1200 B.C., a tribe called simply the "Peoples of the Sea" arrived on the coast. Historians are not certain where they came from, although they may have originated in the lands surrounding the Aegean Sea. These immigrants combined with the early inhabitants of Lebanon to make up the Phoenician people. From 1200 to 334 B.C., the Phoenicians dominated the culture and commerce of their world.

From Sidon, Beirut, Tyre, and the Phoenician capital of Byblos, the sea-faring Phoenicians roamed the Mediterranean in round-bottomed, 50-oared galleys with enormous sails. They traded their precious cedar and cypress lumber. They took raw bronze and iron and worked them into tools and weapons, discovered how to blow glass, and dyed cloth purple with a rare substance found in sea shells. The Phoenicians became the traveling salesmen of the ancient world.

About 950 B.C. Hiram I, King of Tyre, sent cedar, pine, and cypress logs to his good friend, King David of Israel. Hiram also sent carpenters and stonemasons, and David put these craftsmen to work renovating the city of Jerusalem. Hiram's men constructed several palaces and built the First Temple in Jerusalem. Biblical experts believe this temple may have been modeled after

An old etching of Israel's King Solomon

the temple Hiram built to the Phoenician god Baal Melqart in Tyre. Legend says that the porch roof of this fabulous pagan house of worship was supported by a huge column of pure gold and another of solid emerald. Hiram later supplied materials and craftsmen to King David's son, King Solomon.

Some historians believe the Phoenicians sailed to India and England and may even have visited America more than 2,000 years before Columbus set sail. About 600 B.C., on an expedition paid for by the Egyptian Pharaoh Necho II, Phoenician mariners sailed completely around Africa, a feat that would not be duplicated for another 20 centuries. They were also first-class sea warriors, who fought in the service of Xerxes, king of Persia, against the Greeks. Later they steered their horse-headed ships against the Romans.

The Phoenicians grew rich and prosperous from their daring voyages, and those with whom they traded were equally enriched. The brilliant Phoenicians had more than wealth to share with the world. They took the complicated Egyptian alphabet, simplified it into 22 symbols, and gave it to both the Greeks and the Romans. This Phoenician alphabet is the basis of the alphabet used today to write English and most European languages. Phoenicians wrote out their alphabet on shards of broken pottery and on papyrus, the reed paper that they received in trade from the Egyptians. Papyrus is so closely associated with the Phoenician capital of Byblos that when the Greeks translated the writings of the Hebrew prophets, they called the resulting work "the Bible," which comes from "Byblos." Unfortunately, the papyrus docu-

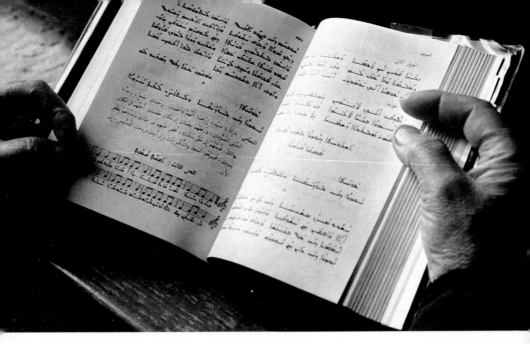

The Bible (shown here in Arabic script) takes its name from Byblos

ments of the Phoenicians rotted away, and the only surviving accounts of the Lords of the Sea are those written by their enemies.

In the case of the Phoenician city of Carthage, the enemies were highly critical. Around 814 B.C., the Phoenicians sent an expedition of colonists to what is today Tunis, on the coast of North Africa. They built a huge and powerful city-state named Carthage. Over the years, the Carthaginians discarded much of the Phoenician heritage and created their own culture. Historians believe that the Carthaginians kept only one Phoenician religious rite: the sacrifice of living infants to their gods. A priest would cut the throat of a baby and then throw the child's body into a blazing

31

fire, while all around the people danced and sang.

The Romans became bitter enemies of the Carthaginians and fought three wars against them. These wars became known as the Punic Wars (Punic is a derivation of "Phoenikes," the Greek word for Phoenicians). The Punic Wars raged from 264 until 146 B.C., when Rome finally triumphed. The hatred between the Romans and the Carthaginians was so strong that the victorious Romans burned Carthage to the ground, plowed under its remains, and then salted the earth so nothing would ever grow there again.

The razing of Carthage is considered the end of the Golden Era of the Phoenicians. After a thousand years of tireless productivity and diplomatic genius, the Phoenicians succumbed to Alexander the Great's army from the east and the Romans from the west. But although their forebears are gone, the Lebanese continue the Phoenician tradition of being the traders and bankers of the Middle East. Despite the current war, Lebanon remains a buffer zone between opposites: east and west, capitalism and socialism, religious fundamentalism and tolerance.

An old engraving depicts the Romans besieging Carthage

*Baalbek is the site of
many Roman ruins*

A Conquered People

In the first century B.C., the prosperous Phoenician city-states were conquered by Rome and incorporated into the larger territory of Syria. Under efficient Roman rule, these city-states became even more important in the Middle East, thriving as trade centers and bridges between cultures. Copper, incense, perfume, famous Phoenician timber, and manufactured goods from the coastal cities continued to be sold all over the known world. Tradesmen, scholars, lawyers, poets, and writers came to Beirut, Byblos, Tyre, and Sidon to share their talents. The city of Baalbek, originally called Heliopolis, became the trading center of the fertile Bekaa Valley in central Lebanon. Scientists who study the Roman ruins of Baalbek believe it was also the center of worship of Roman and Greek gods.

Roman rule came to an end in 634 A.D., however, when the Arabs conquered Syria and the Phoenician territories. The Arab conquest was fueled by a new and powerful religion that was sweeping the Middle East. The history of the world would be forever changed by this new religion, Islam.

Islam originated in 613 A.D., when the prophet Muhammad had a religious awakening. Muhammad believed that God had revealed to him the one true faith, a new religion that combined the tenets of both Christianity and Judaism. For a few years, Muhammad shared his revelation only with close friends and relatives, but soon this new religion—which Muhammad called Islam—began to take hold throughout his native city of Mecca, in what is now Saudi Arabia. Filled with religious fervor, Muhammad's followers (called Muslims) united into a huge army to spread the message of Islam across the Middle East.

Although the number of Muslims was small, their strong religious beliefs carried them forward. During a 30-year period, they made one conquest after another. By 642, the Muslims controlled Mesopotamia, Syria, Palestine, Egypt, Persia, and half of Spain. Until 711, when it was defeated by the Franks at the Battle of Tours, the Islamic army threatened to conquer all of Europe. Although it failed to dominate the entire European continent, the Muslim Empire spread from the edge of India to the Atlantic Ocean. The ancient city-states of Phoenicia came under Muslim control, and the Arab conquerors shifted power away from the city-states to the Syrian cities of Aleppo, Hana, and Damascus.

Although they had lost their political power, Sidon, Tyre, Byblos, and Beirut continued to exert a strong commercial and cultural influence on the world. When the huge Arab army disbanded, many of its soldiers remained in Lebanon, attracted by opportunities for making money and for farming in the Bekaa Valley. More and more Arabs migrated to the old Phoenician settlements from other parts of the Middle East, bringing with them their own language and customs.

The Romans decorated their temples with colorful mosaics

This arch dates from the time of Christ

37

*Maronite Christian
monks uphold
centuries of
tradition*

A small sect of rebellious Christians remained resistant to Muslim religion and law. They called themselves Maronites, after Maron, a Christian monk. These Christians hid from the Muslims in the rugged Lebanon Mountains, as the early Christians had hidden from Roman soldiers hundreds of years before. The Maronites entrenched themselves in the northern part of the country, where they survived and prospered.

European Christians were bitter about the loss of the Holy Land to the Muslims. For one thing, it meant that Europeans could no longer make pilgrimages to the sacred shrines of Jesus. The European powers decided, therefore, to mount military expeditions—called Crusades—to reclaim the land. In 1095, Pope Urban II proclaimed the First Crusade. His aim was not only to

38

restore the Holy Land to the Church, but to distract feudal armies from the warfare that was tearing Europe apart.

Thousands of Europeans participated in the Crusades. Many of the Crusaders were kings, princes, dukes, bishops, and earls. Some of them, though, were peasants, shopkeepers, and artisans who sought to make money from the wars. In the course of 12 Crusades between the 11th and 13th centuries, control of the holy places shifted back and forth between Muslims and Christians. In 1291, however, the Crusaders lost their last battle and were driven back to Europe.

The Crusaders left behind many remarkable fortresses that today are Lebanese landmarks, and they returned to Europe with

An etching of Pope Urban II urging the Crusaders in 1095

The Crusader Castle still stands in Jebeil

a taste for such Middle Eastern fare as sesame seeds, carob beans, rice, lentils, lemons, melons, apricots, and shallots. They also carried back to Europe a love of martial games, tournaments, and heraldic decorations that would form the base of chivalry in the coming Middle Ages. Europeans had discovered Persian rugs and tapestries, glass mirrors and face powder, and brilliant dyes such as carmine and lilac. They demanded more and more of these goods. The task of exporting all of this exotic booty to the great cities of the West was won, of course, by the merchants of Lebanon. By the end of the 13th century, Tyre, Sidon, Byblos, and Beirut, now firmly Arab, were thriving once again.

Shortly after the Crusaders were pushed back to Europe, a group of former slaves seized power in Egypt. These conquerors, known as the Mamelukes, ruled Egypt until 1517. While they governed Egypt, the Mamelukes allied themselves with a powerful Lebanese clan, the Buhturs. Through this association, the Mamelukes were able to control Lebanon as well. They allowed the Maronite Christians, who had forged strong links with their fellow Catholics during the era of the Crusades, to rule in their own territories. The Mamelukes also permitted the Druze, a mysterious religious sect whose beliefs were based loosely on Islam, to govern themselves.

The Mamelukes were driven from Lebanon in 1517, when the Ottoman (Turkish) Empire conquered the territory. The Ottomans had controlled parts of Turkey, Greece, Egypt, Libya, Tunis, Hungary, and other territories since the 14th century. For the next four centuries, they would also rule Lebanon.

During the Ottoman reign, a great Lebanese leader came to power. Fahkr al-Din M'an, born in 1591, is considered the Father of Modern Lebanon. Although he lived to be only 42 years old, M'an greatly advanced Lebanese culture and economy. He sought European advice on improving manufacturing techniques, and he imported Italian farmers to modernize agriculture. Most important, however, Fakhr al-Din M'an formed alliances between the feuding Maronite Christians and the Druze. Although he was a Druze, M'an encouraged the industrious Maronites to move to the southern part of Lebanon to learn the silk-making trade. He taught the Lebanese that only when people of all religions cooperated in politics and business could the country survive and prosper. Slowly, he became the most powerful man in the country and steered Lebanon away from the influence of foreign powers.

By the mid-1620s, however, the Turks began to feel threatened by M'an's power. They drove him into exile in Tuscany, where he gathered an army and waged war against the Ottomans. In 1633, Fahkr al-Din M'an was captured in battle and put to death in Constantinople, the capital of the Ottoman Empire. But by 1667 his grand-nephew, Ahmad M'an, had restored the family power over southern and central Lebanon.

The Lebanon of the 17th century was under foreign influence. When Ahmad M'an died in 1697 without leaving a direct heir, the Ottomans decided that political power should pass to the Druze. Soon, however, the head of the most important Druze clan embraced Christianity, and the Maronite Catholics became the leading political and economic force in the country.

The ruins of the Temple of Reslief in Byblos

Lebanon's varied religious groups lived together peacefully for some time. But peace in Lebanon was shattered in the mid-1800s, when Christian peasants rose up against their Christian overlords in a series of violent land disputes. Because there were many Christians living in Druze areas, Druze feudal chiefs attempted to suppress the Christian uprising. Violent clashes between Christians and Druze became commonplace. Then, in the early 1860s, a group of Druze massacred more than 11,000 Maronite peasants.

Moved by loyalty to their fellow Christians, the French government intervened and demanded that the Ottomans restore the peace. Under European pressure, the Ottoman overlords devised a new government. Lebanon had been governed under a feudal system, in which peasants were obligated to an overlord for protection. The new system introduced wide-ranging laws. A national police force was organized, citizens were guaranteed certain rights, and members of governing councils were elected.

Despite the new government, Lebanon remained divided by religious and cultural differences. While most Muslims adhered strictly to Arab customs and cultures, Christians became increasingly westernized. Many young Maronite men traveled to Rome to study for the priesthood of the Catholic Church. They returned with news of inventions, literature, scientific progress, and fashion. The Lebanese taste for a more European lifestyle increased. Because the Christians lived in close contact with the Muslims, Western thoughts and ideas eventually spread to the Muslims as well. The strict religious laws that dominated life in other Islamic

Musseiliba Castle,
built in the 1600s

states became more and more lax in Lebanon.

By the turn of the century, Catholic and Protestant missionaries were flocking to Lebanon to preach their gospels and establish church-run schools. Newspapers and books circulated widely, and French, English, and Italian words and phrases found their way into the Arabic language. Many Lebanese abandoned traditional Arab clothing and adopted European-style dress.

By 1915, Lebanon had become the crown jewel of the Turkish Ottoman Empire. After World War I, however, the status of Lebanon changed radically. During the war, the Ottoman Turks allied themselves with Germany. When the Germans were defeated, the Turks lost all their territories, including Lebanon. In 1918, the League of Nations (an organization of countries similar to the present United Nations) determined that Lebanon would be governed by France. This commission to govern a territory or country was called a mandate. At the end of World War I, many Middle Eastern countries were mandated, including Palestine, Syria, Iraq, and Egypt.

The French mandate brought direct benefits to Lebanon. In 1926, the first Lebanese constitution was approved, and the country's name was formally changed to The Republic of Lebanon. When a Maronite was elected president in 1934, a tradition was established; since then, all Lebanese presidents have been Christians, and all prime ministers have been Muslim. Under an unwritten "gentleman's agreement," seats in the Chamber of Deputies were divided between Christians and Muslims, as were positions in other government and community agencies.

Turkish dress was worn during the Ottoman period

Brides wore red gowns and headpieces made of coins

46

On November 26, 1941, Lebanon proclaimed its independence from France, and by 1946 all French troops had been withdrawn. But the transition from mandated nation to independent Arab republic did not go smoothly. The terms of the first two presidents ended in turmoil. In 1958, opposition to President Camille Chamoun by Muslim supporters of Egyptian President Gamal Nasser was so strong that it threatened to topple the government. Chamoun asked United States President Dwight Eisenhower to send troops to restore order, and on July 15 a large contingent of United States marines and soldiers waded onto the beaches of Beirut from landing craft offshore. For the first time, the United States had been drawn into the internal political strife of Lebanon.

American forces left Lebanon in October, 1958, but peace did not endure. Christians and Muslims skirmished constantly until 1975, when the stage was set for full-blown civil war.

U.S. Marines have been sent to Lebanon twice in the past 30 years

War Without End

Since 1975, more than 80,000 Lebanese have been killed and more than 40,000 children orphaned in a bloody civil war. Several factors contributed to Lebanon's status as one of the most seriously troubled countries in the world.

For many years, Lebanese Muslims—who make up the majority of the population—have resented the extreme influence and power given to the Christian minority after the French left Lebanon in 1946. This problem was made even more severe in 1948, when the partition of Palestine sent a flood of homeless Palestinian Muslims into Lebanon. Because Lebanon had a population of only 2,000,000 people, the addition of 400,000 Palestinians gave the Muslims an even greater majority. Furthermore, Lebanon was unequipped to offer jobs and housing to such a large number of refugees. The Palestinians were forced to live in squalid tent-cities on the outskirts of Beirut and other Lebanese towns.

Then, in the early 1970s, a series of events in the neighboring Kingdom of Jordan caused further trouble for Lebanon. Many Palestinian refugees had settled in Jordan. In the early 1970s, Jordan became the base for the Palestine Liberation Organization (PLO), a group dedicated to regaining—often through violence—land that had been lost in the 1948 partition of Palestine. After a series of violent clashes between the forces of Jordan's King Hussein and the *fedayeen* (commandos) of the PLO, the Palestinians were driven from Jordan. These Palestinians, many of whom had been on the move for 25 years, joined their fellow countrymen in the miserable refugee camps of Lebanon. Today, more than 500,000 Palestinians live in these crowded tent-cities.

This surge of refugees had two effects on Lebanon. First, it created a sudden increase of Muslims, threatening the unsteady alliance between Christians and Muslims. Second, the PLO fedayeen began to recruit commandos from among the unemployed, displaced Palestinian youth. Many of these young commandos took part in terrorist raids into Israel. In turn, Israeli planes fiercely attacked the tent settlements in southern Lebanon. The fedayeen also began skirmishing with the regular Lebanese government forces, made up mostly of Christians. The president of

Displaced, impoverished Palestinians live in makeshift camps

Lebanon blamed the PLO for the increasingly frequent deaths of innocent civilians in these raids and guerilla attacks.

Soon—in addition to the fedayeen, the regular Lebanese army, and a number of Palestinian splinter groups—both Muslim and Christian groups established private armies (militias) of their own. These opposing forces began clashing in Beirut.

One more element has contributed to the conflict in Lebanon. While few Arab states were as westernized as Lebanon, many of them had become lax in enforcing the laws of the Prophet Muhammad as contained in the Koran, the sacred book of the Muslims. Throughout the 1970s, however, the idea of a return to the fundamental beliefs of Islam began to spread across the Middle East. Many Muslims began to envision a renewed unity of the Arabic-speaking world, linked by religion, language, and culture. The notion of a more strictly religious Middle East and of Arab unity took root in Iran, where the shah was deposed by the Ayatollah Khomeini and his *mullahs* (Islamic priests). Gradually, other Muslim nations began embracing the old ways: strict obedience to religious law, Arab-style clothing, and the like. Lebanon, with its Christian president and links to Christian Western Europe, was seen as an obstacle to Arab unity and renewed Muslim faith. As a result, pressure was applied by Middle Eastern states to the fragile, Christian-controlled government of Lebanon.

Open warfare was sparked in April 1975, when a bus carrying Palestinians was attacked by a Christian militia in East Beirut. PLO forces joined with Muslim militias to fight Christian militias and government forces—and the war was on. Battles were fought

An explosion rocked Beirut when oil tanks were bombed in 1978

in downtown Beirut, scattering tourists, office workers, and farmers on their way to market.

In late 1976, the Lebanese government asked Syrian forces to step in to separate the warring Christians and Muslims. By mid-1978, most of the fighting had stopped. Then, shooting erupted between the Syrians and the Christian militias; this conflict continued until 1981.

A cease-fire negotiated by United States Special Envoy Philip C. Habib (an American of Lebanese descent) ended after ten months in 1982, when the PLO attempted to assassinate the Israeli ambassador in London. The Israelis retaliated with air attacks against PLO strongholds in southern Lebanon. The PLO, in turn, responded with rocket attacks into cities in northern Israel.

Finally, the Israeli army, under General Ariel Sharon, marched into Lebanon, reaching and laying siege to Beirut in mid-June. Israeli forces encircled PLO and Syrian forces within the city for two-and-one-half months, pounding them with air, sea, and artillery bombardment. Ambassador Habib negotiated the release of the trapped Syrian and Palestinian fighters, and in August 1982, they were evacuated.

Then, on September 14, 1982, only nine days before he was to take office as president of Lebanon, Bashir Gemayel was assassinated by a bomb while he was speaking to a meeting in East Beirut. Three days later, vengeful Christian militiamen entered the Sabra and Shatila refugee camps in West Beirut and—allegedly in retaliation for Gemayel's death—massacred hundreds of Palestinian men, women, and children.

On September 21, Bashir Gemayel's brother, Amine, was unanimously elected president by the National Assembly. He took office two days later, declaring he would restore peace and prosperity to Lebanon. In February of 1983, the United States, France, Britain, and Italy sent troops to attempt to separate the combatants once and for all. Nevertheless, the fighting continued, and in Octo-

PLO soldiers left Beirut in 1982

ber a car bomb destroyed the United States Marine barracks, killing dozens of soldiers. Following this incident, a number of French soldiers were killed in bomb blasts. Two years later, the foreign powers withdrew their forces. Since then, one cease-fire after another has been declared—only to be broken hours later.

Despite the cry for Arab unity, Muslims have not found unity easy to achieve, especially in Beirut. At least a dozen Muslim militias and terrorist groups disagree violently with each other's philosophies and goals. Many of them owe allegiance to Syria, Iran, Iraq, or Libya, and all of them add to the confusion of just who is fighting whom in Lebanon's bloody puzzle of factions, religions, and foreign powers. One terrorist group, for example, hijacked a TWA flight in July of 1985 and then surrendered custody of the plane to another group when it landed at Beirut airport. Yet a third group negotiated the release of the hostage passengers. Finally, a fourth Muslim militia took credit for the event.

Lebanon's current political troubles cannot be easily understood, and they will not be easily solved. Yet this ancient country and its diverse people and cultures have remarkable powers of endurance and much to offer the rest of the world.

Foreign troops guarded Beirut's airport

The People of Lebanon

The Lebanese people are diverse a mix of many cultures and national origins. Every nation that has conquered this country has woven its culture into the fabric of Lebanese life. Over the centuries, however, the Arabs have contributed most to the physical, emotional, and cultural characteristics of the Lebanese. Today,

Lebanese farmers proudly display their wares at a village market

fully 93 percent of Lebanese people are of Arab ancestry, about 6 percent are Armenian, and 1 percent are ethnically mixed.

Most Lebanese have dark skin and black or dark brown hair. Like other Semitic people, many Lebanese have large noses, high cheekbones, and dark eyes inherited from the desert Arabs of the 8th century who swept through the Middle East as soldiers in Muhammad's Islamic army.

All Lebanese speak Arabic. As a result of the 23-year mandate by France, many of them speak French as well. In fact, a large percentage of the population is trilingual: in any major city of Lebanon, ordinary men and women can speak Arabic, French, and English. As the bankers and merchants of the Middle East, the Lebanese learned centuries ago that they must communicate with foreigners. Learning second and even third languages is taken very much for granted.

Lebanese Hospitality

Because it is the trade center of the Middle East, Lebanon has had much experience dealing with strangers and foreigners. Lebanese people make a virtue of warm hospitality, and even the humblest household will offer a visitor a cup of bitter, black Arabic coffee or some tea with fresh mint sprigs. Hospitality is so highly valued that many Lebanese adhere to the "three-time" rule: a guest must be offered refreshment at least three times before the host can accept his refusal.

Much of Lebanese social life centers around the drinking of Arabic coffee, considered the national drink. The Lebanese claim

Lebanon's architecture combines Arabic and Western motifs

it tastes best when it is slurped. No stranger, friend, or relative has been properly welcomed to a Lebanese home until he has been offered this traditional coffee, which is served in tiny cups. Arabic coffee leaves a residue of fine black grounds in the bottom of the cup, and some Lebanese believe that a person's fortune can be read by deciphering the shapes and symbols found in the coffee grounds.

Another Lebanese beverage is *arak*, an anise-flavored liqueur. Although arak is clear in color, it turns a milky white when water or ice is added. Arak is sold all over Lebanon, but many Lebanese prefer to make their own at home.

The ceremonious preparation of food is an important part of the Lebanese way of life. *Kibbeh*—a kind of meatloaf made from lamb and *burghal* (crushed wheat)—is considered the national dish. To make kibbeh, lamb and burghal are placed in a stone mortar and kneaded for about an hour. The mixture is seasoned with garlic and cooked, although true connoisseurs say it's best eaten raw. Other Lebanese specialties include *mehshee* (lamb and rice rolled in grape leaves) and *hoomus* (a dip made from chickpeas and sesame paste and served with flat Arabic bread). And no traditional Lebanese meal is complete without a dessert of *buhlawa*, a sticky pastry made with honey and walnuts, or *namora*, a semolina-and-honey cake.

The Family

Nothing is more important to a Lebanese than his family. Loyalty to the family—even to distant relatives—is the most important value in Lebanese life. The Lebanese expect loyalty not only from their immediate family, but from in-laws and distant relations. Their concept of family is so strong that even Lebanese who are not related often refer to one another as cousin.

Many times, related families become political clans, ruling a local area or a town and in some cases rising to high government office. Lebanon's current president, Amine Gemayel, took office after his brother, Bashir, was assassinated by a bomb in 1982. Until his death in 1985, the Gemayels' father, Pierre, was the most influential political figure in all Lebanon and leader of the Maronite Catholic faction. The Gemayel family is a good example of how the extreme closeness of Lebanese families can sometimes build a political dynasty.

Even Lebanese who immigrate to other countries—and since the war began many have done so, relocating to such faraway

Bashir Gemayel was heir to a dynasty

places as Australia and Brazil—remain devoted to their families in the motherland. Once they leave their native country, however, most Lebanese emigrants do not return, except for vacations. Nevertheless, they maintain strong emotional ties with their homeland, and the Lebanese economy is in part dependent upon the millions of dollars that Lebanese emigrants send back to their families. Today, more people of Lebanese ancestry live outside of Lebanon than within it. In the United States alone, there are 100,000 Lebanese immigrants and more than two million people of Lebanese ancestry. In 1960, an organization called the World Lebanese Union was founded to help Lebanese families who have left their homeland keep track of one another.

Although women are guaranteed equal rights under the Lebanese constitution, men dominate the society. Most Lebanese believe that a woman's primary place is in the home, and there is still great separation of the sexes: Lebanese men spend most of their time with other men, while women stay at home, rearing the children and preparing meals. Although Lebanese women have the right to vote and can hold public office, no woman has ever held an important government post. In the last few decades, how-ever, more and more Lebanese women have turned away from domestic life and are becoming lawyers, teachers, and doctors.

Daily Life

Every Lebanese town has its own *suq*, a market where merchants pile their stalls high with fruits and vegetables, manufactured goods, and clothing. The suq is always found in the oldest part of the city or town, and it is usually an enclosed area filled with merchandise and fragrant with the smells of exotic foods and incense. Each tiny shop in the suq has its own specialty: leather goods, metal plates, souvenirs, or traditional *caftans* (the long dresses sometimes worn by both men and women in the Middle East). A chaos of signs, awnings, pots, food, and people fills the suq with intense confusion. Much of the noise comes from buyers

Beirutians haggle over fruits and vegetables at this colorful suq

and sellers haggling over prices, a custom most Americans find intimidating. But Lebanese, like all Middle Easterners, believe that the cost of an item can always be bartered down—and they're always right.

One item that can be purchased at any suq in Lebanon is *misbaha*, or "worry beads." All over the country, one hears the clicking of these strings of small stone beads. The Lebanese "worry" away impatience, boredom, hostility, or nervousness by turning the beads over and over in their hands, sometimes fiddling with them for hours. They say the misbaha keep them from losing their tempers or showing too much emotion—a necessity in a country beset by hostilities.

The Lebanese tolerance for new ideas is evident in their style of dress. City-dwelling Lebanese, especially those in Beirut, love fashionable clothing and consider themselves the best-dressed of all Arab populations. In fact, new clothing trends from Europe reach Beirut long before they become known in the United States. Lebanese from rural, less affluent areas wear western-style clothing, usually a shirt and trousers for the men and a loose-fitting dress for women. Older women may wear dark scarves over their heads, but few Lebanese Muslim women wear the *chador*, the long black robe that covers all but the eyes of women in strict Muslim countries such as Iran and Saudi Arabia.

The population of Lebanon contains an unusually large percentage of young people, because the birth rate is high and fewer infants are killed by disease than in other Arab countries. The average Lebanese lives about 65 years. The country's population

During cease-fires, Lebanese citizens crowd the streets of Beirut

has been estimated to be approximately 3.1 million, a figure that would probably reach 4 million if the many Palestinian refugees in Lebanon were included. Most Lebanese live in urban areas, particularly in Beirut and Tripoli. In 1970, 50 percent of the total population lived in Beirut, although the war has forced many people into the countryside. The Bekaa Valley is the least populated part of Lebanon. Nonstop warfare has made an accurate census impossible, and all population figures are at best rough estimates.

A Conflict of Religions

A number of Lebanon's problems stem from conflicting religious beliefs. The variety of religions that makes Lebanon one of the most distinctive countries in the Middle East also causes strife.

61

Lebanon has 17 recognized religious sects. It's not surprising that so many faiths are represented; for centuries Lebanon has been the link between Christian Europe, Jewish Palestine, Muslim Africa and Arabia, Asia Minor, and parts of Asia. And the Lebanon Mountains, with their rough terrain and impassable ridges, have traditionally been the hiding place for persecuted believers from every corner of the Middle East.

Of the 40 percent of Lebanese who are Christian, more than half are Maronite Catholics. The rest are Orthodox Catholics of

The Church of St. John in Byblos, built by Crusaders in 1100 A.D.

Byzantine rite or Melkites (Greek Catholics). Some 58 percent of Lebanese follow some form of Islam.

The majority of Lebanese Muslims are of the Shi'ite sect. Shi'ites believe that the Prophet Muhammad's son-in-law, Ali, was his true successor (*Imam*). Members of the second largest Muslim sect—the Sunni Muslims—are distinguished from the Shi'ites because they do not believe that Ali was the Imam.

One of the smallest religious groups in Lebanon is the Druze sect. Although their religion began as an offshoot of Islam, the Druze no longer consider themselves Muslims. They practice their faith in secret according to the rules of their holy book, known as *al-Hikma* (The Book of Wisdom). There are only about 215,000 Druze in Lebanon, but they exert a political influence far greater than their numbers would suggest, largely because of the power attained by Fahkr al-Din M'an in the 17th century.

Most of the remaining Lebanese belong to other Islamic sects. In addition, about 1,000 Jews live in Lebanon, most of them in Beirut. There are also some small communities of Protestant Christians scattered throughout the country.

Beirut: City Under Siege

Lebanon has five principal cities: Beirut (population 1.1 million), Tripoli (240,000), Sidon (110,000), Tyre (60,000), and Zahlah (55,000). Beirut, the capital, is the most spectacular. Over the centuries, this ancient Phoenician city-state has kept pace with new urban developments. By 1975, high-rise hotels, apartments, and office buildings jammed Beirut's broad boulevards and pictur-

In 1982, Israeli troops moved their tanks into Muslim West Beirut

esque hillsides. The entire Arab world seemed to be investing its millions in the real estate, corporations, and international banks of Beirut. The latest in electronic gear and other consumer goods—as well as ideas, trends, and knowledge-came through its port at a staggering rate. In the evenings, wealthy Arab investors and Lebanese intellectuals argued politics and money at the fashionable Cafe Chilicie or in the Hotel St. Georges.

Unfortunately, civil war has changed the way of life in Beirut. Many hotels are now rubble. Rooftop snipers with rifles drive sunbathers and swimmers from the beaches. The outdoor cafes have moved indoors to avoid curbside car bombs, and the millions of tourists who once flocked to Lebanon's resorts now vacation elsewhere. The city of Beirut is divided along an imaginary "Green Line": Muslims on the west, Christians on the east.

The deluxe hotels—the St. Georges, the Phoenicia Intercontinental, the Hilton, and the Holiday Inn—that dotted the popular Ramlet el Baida beach were the sites of some of the fiercest fighting in the late 1970s. Later, they were bombed into rubble by Israeli war planes during the invasion of 1982. Today, fighting is constant in many parts of Beirut; in certain neighborhoods, even a trip to the grocery store is risky. Although cease-fires are often declared, they are usually broken within a few hours. Gunfire is heard day and night.

Recently, however, another sound has been heard in Beirut: the rumble of bulldozers and steam shovels scooping up the rubble and digging deep foundations for new and better hotels, shops, and restaurants. Even in the midst of heavy fighting, most

65

In the 1960s, Beirut's skyline glittered with modern architecture

Lebanese remain more loyal to Beirut than to the factions that threaten to destroy it. These loyal Lebanese are trying to rebuild their city.

Some sections of Beirut retain traces of their former elegance. The regal Summerland Hotel is once again accepting guests, even though hotel employees must step over gaping holes in the upper floors as they show visitors to their rooms. The shops of Rue Hamra offer the latest French and Italian designer clothes. When the shelling stops, Beirutians jump into their cars and rush about their business, jamming traffic on the street Corniche Mazraa.

Until 1982, when the PLO mined the track against the invading Israeli army, the Hippodrome racetrack was where Beirutians of all religious beliefs bet on their favorite horses each day. Today, movies are the most popular form of entertainment in Beirut. According to a survey taken by the United Nations, the city has the tenth highest movie-going population in the world.

Investors call Beirut the Switzerland of the Middle East. Like Switzerland, it has free economic and foreign exchange systems, favorable interest rates, and banking secrecy laws. Today, there are 95 banks and investment companies in the city—14 more than when fighting began. While the war has destroyed the tourist industry, banking and finance at least continue to thrive.

Rubble is being cleared from Beirut and carted off to a landfill by the sea. The garbage is collected every week, the electricity is on, and the telephones work. Private businessmen are investing millions of dollars of their own money to bring Beirut back to life. Many people, however, doubt that the city can ever be restored to its former glory. Beirut is older than Rome, perhaps older even than Athens; Egyptian scribes noted its existence as early as the 15th century B.C., and it probably was not young then. The people of Beirut now worry that their ancient city may not survive 20th-century turmoil and modern warfare.

The Summerland
Hotel is a posh resort

War is a part of everyday life for Palestinian refugee children

Government and Economy

Lebanon is a republic with a parliamentary system of government. Its constitution was established in 1926 and is modeled on that of the Third French Republic, which mandated the country at the time. Later amendments have changed the constitution. The most important amendment is Article 95, which calls for equitable distribution of government posts among the various religious sects. The 99-member National Assembly is organized on a religious basis: the assembly must have a ratio of six Christians to every five Muslims, making the total number always a multiple of eleven.

The National Assembly is elected by popular vote every four years. Because of the fighting, however, there have been no elections since 1972. Instead, the last elected assembly has been extended, but it has been active only occasionally since 1975.

National Assembly members elect the president by a two-thirds majority for a six-year term. According to unwritten law, the president must be a Maronite Catholic, the prime minister a Sunni Muslim, and the president of the National Assembly a Shi'ite Muslim.

Under the constitution, the president is the most powerful person in the country. He appoints the Cabinet of Ministers and

U.S. Marines tried to keep the peace in war-torn Beirut

selects the prime minister. The president also has the power to enforce the laws of the National Assembly, to negotiate and ratify treaties, and to propose new laws to the Assembly.

While United States politicians belong to political parties, Lebanese politicians are divided into religious factions. As in England, which also has a parliamentary system, the Assembly can call on the prime minister or cabinet to answer questions or demand a vote of confidence, although this rarely happens. Most cabinets lose power because the members disagree among themselves or because the president withdraws his support.

The judicial system of Lebanon is modeled on the Napoleonic Code of France (laws devised and instituted by the Emperor Napoleon when he ruled France in the early 19th century). There are no jury trials in Lebanon; judges decide guilt or innocence. Each court has three levels of judicial appeal, and there are also religious courts that deal with personal matters such as marriage, inheritance, and property.

Lebanon is divided into six *muhafazat* (provinces): Bayrut (Beirut), Jabel Lubnan, ash-Shamal, al Janub, al-Bekaa, and an-Nabatiah. Each province is administered by a *muhafiz* (governor) appointed by the Ministry of the Interior for a four-year term.

The Lebanese Economy

Lebanon is one of the few countries in the world that has based its economy on services rather than on manufactured goods or natural resources. The Lebanese economy successfully combines tradition and progress; as in the days of the Phoenicians, foreign trade is very important. Today, however, the Lebanese no longer export timber and import gold. The most important exports now are fruit and vegetables, building materials, textiles and clothing, and electrical equipment. The major imports are crude petroleum, chemicals, textiles, machinery, automobiles, household appliances, and food.

Many Lebanese work in their homes, especially since the war has destroyed office buildings and industrial areas. And many do the same work that their fathers and grandfathers did before them.

Lebanon exports much of its produce

Villages and small towns produce specialty items: hand-tied rugs, copper trays and utensils, or hand-loomed silks. Some villages have become famous for products or features uniquely their own. For instance, Al Fakyah is known for its rugs, Al Batrun for lemonade, Jazzin for cutlery, Al Mina for fried fish, and Rashin for sculpture.

The country is not rich in natural resources. Its only large deposits are of limestone and high-quality sand, used for making glass. It also has small amounts of iron ore, asphalt, coal, and phosphates. Lebanon's chief natural resource has always been its dense forests. Lebanese cedar and cypress have been logged since the days of the Phoenicians, and much of the forest land is now barren. A few decades ago, Lebanese officials—recalling that their country once boasted the greatest forests in the Middle East—decided to plant thousands of seedlings, hoping to restore the towering cypress trees to the hillsides. This effort, known as the "Green Plan," has been stalled due to the war, but some small groves of trees now flourish in the mountains.

Because soil in Lebanon is poor, many Lebanese have studied in American agricultural schools to learn how to improve it. New agricultural techniques have paid off. Bananas, citrus fruit, and vegetables are grown on the coastal plain, and olives, grapes, tobacco, figs, and almonds flourish in the foothills. At elevations of 1,500 feet (450 meters), peaches, plums, cherries, and apricots thrive. Apples and pears grow at higher elevations. Chickens and other poultry have increased the income of Lebanese farmers. Livestock is less important here than in other parts of the Middle

The cedar's cones
stand upright

East, although sheep, cattle, and goats are kept. Farms are extremely small, however, and fewer Lebanese become farmers with each generation, despite improvements in agricultural science.

Industry has suffered greatly since the civil war began. Many industrial areas, including the Shuwayfat section of southeast Beirut, which before the war was a manufacturing center, have been destroyed by artillery shelling and bombs. Before hostilities interfered, the chief industries of Lebanon were textile production, food processing, plywood and furniture manufacturing, and printing. The chemical, pharmaceutical, and aluminum industries had begun to thrive, but they have been more or less shut down by the war.

Banking and finance remain the most important elements of the Lebanese economy. Of the 72 officially recognized banks, 35 are Lebanese, 18 are Lebanese with foreign participation, and 19 are foreign. The country's currency unit is the Lebanese *pound*. The monetary system is based on the decimal system (built on units of 10 and 100). Just as there are 100 pennies in a United

73

Even city-dwelling Lebanese keep small animals such as goats, seen here on a Beirut street

States dollar, there are 100 *piasters* in a Lebanese pound. One Lebanese pound is equal in value to about 30 United States cents.

Lebanese are by nature a hardworking people, and they have built their economy into one of the richest in the Middle East. Unlike many Middle Eastern nations, Lebanon has a large middle class. It is possible for a Lebanese born in poverty to become prosperous and successful. In 1951, the average yearly income was equivalent to only 250 United States dollars; today, it averages about 1,500 dollars.

Although many Lebanese still earn their living through agriculture and commerce, as their ancestors did centuries ago, only 11 percent of the population are farmers, compared to 20 percent in 1970. Agriculture represents just 9 percent of Lebanon's gross national product, or GNP (the combination of all goods and services produced in the country in a year). More than half of all Lebanese now work in the industrial labor force, which produces approximately 13 percent of the GNP. The country's industrial sites include three cement factories, two oil refineries, and two steel mills.

The remainder of the Lebanese work force is engaged in trade and services, although the destruction of the port of Beirut, the airport's insecure status, and the heavy damage to beachfront hotels and restaurants have critically hurt these activities.

Development of industry, housing, telecommunications, roads, and the water supply system has virtually halted since 1975. Experts estimate that if the fighting stopped today, it would take 10 years and 12 billion dollars to rebuild the country.

The banking district in prewar Beirut

Education, Communication, Transportation

When the Ottoman Turks ruled Lebanon, they did little to educate the populace. When the Turks retreated from Lebanon after World War I, however, education was taken over by French Catholic clergy and by British and American Protestant missionaries. Soon, Muslim denominations and other religious organizations set up

Yachts are moored at the marina in Jouneih, a wealthy resort town

their own schools. Almost overnight, a private education equal to the best in Europe was available in Lebanon.

For a long time, these private schools bore the burden of educating Lebanon's children. The public school system was poor, so few Lebanese attended state-sponsored schools. By 1970, however, the government began taking responsibility for education. More children began attending public schools, and the courses of study at public schools were revised. Still, most Lebanese agree that the best education is found in private schools.

Education in Lebanon consists of a five-year primary school which all children must attend. Primary school is followed by a seven-year secondary school, after which students may attend either a university or a four-year vocational training school. There are 400,000 children enrolled in school in Lebanon. About 254,000 of them are in secondary schools.

Lebanon has a long history of higher education. In ancient times, the Romans established a law school in Beirut equal to those in Athens and Alexandria. Because of this school, Beirut in ancient times was known as the "Nurse of Laws," which meant that it was a city that nurtured the laws of Rome. Today, Beirut has five universities. The oldest and most prestigious is the American University of Beirut, founded in 1866. Students come from all over the world to attend its classes, which are taught in English. French Jesuit priests founded the University of St. Joseph in 1881. This university is considered to be very influential because many of its graduates have become important politicians and leaders. Lebanese University, founded in 1953, is a state-run college, and the Arab University of Beirut, established in 1960, is an extension of the University of Alexandria in Egypt. The fifth Beirut university is Saint Esprit de Kaslike, opened in 1950.

In addition to these universities, several community colleges offer training in specific fields, including music, teaching, and religion.

Reading, Watching, and Listening

Lebanese people get most of their news and information by reading. The country has nearly 470 periodical publications, 40 of them daily newspapers. This seems like an astounding number for a small country, but it includes publications in Arabic, English, French, and Armenian.

Half of all Lebanese households—about 420,000—have television sets. Two privately owned television stations air a variety of Lebanese shows, as well as some American series dubbed into Arabic. Lebanese viewers can also pick up broadcasts from Syria and Egypt.

Like all Middle Easterners, Lebanese rely heavily on their radios (the country has millions of them) for up-to-the-minute news about the war and world events. The Lebanese are very knowledgeable about world events, and they know how important their tiny country is to both the United States and the Soviet Union. The government-run Lebanese Broadcasting Station broadcasts in Arabic, French, English, and Armenian. In addition, each of the Muslim and Christian militias has its own clandestine radio station. The militias broadcast not only news to their fighters but propaganda to other listeners, hoping to win them over. With so many secret stations broadcasting conflicting stories, it is often impossible to make sense of any of them.

Lebanon is one of the few countries in the Middle East where citizens have freedom of expression. Government censorship is minimal, so most publications operate without restraint of any sort. Because of this, newspapers and magazines in Beirut have been nicknamed the "Parliament of the Arab world." They are the only forum for free and open discussion in the Middle East. All Middle-Eastern problems and issues are debated in their pages.

Transportation

Lebanon is a country on the move. The people are always traveling: to work, to market, or to visit members of their large,

Sidon has been an important port since the days of the Phoenicians

extended families. They use every inch of the 2,500 miles (4,000 kilometers) of roads that cross their country. About 300 miles (480 kilometers) of these roads are part of the international highway that connects the Middle East with both Europe and Asia. Lebanese without private cars use low-cost taxis and buses.

Railways in the Middle East are not as efficient as those in Europe and North America, so they are used mostly by tourists and seldom by local people. One small railway that runs across the Lebanon Mountains, through the Bekaa Valley, and along the Mediterranean coast is especially popular with visitors who want to admire the beautiful Lebanese landscape. A daily passenger train travels from Beirut to the Syrian city of Aleppo, but most Lebanese prefer to drive that route. The majority of Lebanon's railway lines are used to carry bulk cargo.

The ports that made Lebanon famous in ancient times still thrive today. Instead of the cedar boats that carried the Phoenicians around the world, huge oil tankers, each as long as a city block, lie at anchor offshore from Lebanon's oil pipeline terminals.

The chief port is Beirut. Even in the midst of warfare, almost 3,000 ships and 95,000 passengers arrive at or depart from the Port of Beirut each year. The docks, which can hold 20 ships, handle 3.5 million tons of goods per year.

Beirut's airport was once one of the busiest in the Middle East. Today, however, control of the runways and terminals passes back and forth between many of the Muslim militias, and most American and European airlines find it too dangerous to land in Beirut.

Five Thousand Years of Culture

Lebanese culture has borrowed the best from many sources: Phoenician, Greek, Roman, Byzantine, Turkish, and French. But Lebanon is primarily an Arab land and shares many cultural similarities with its Arab neighbors. Because of the country's traditional openness, though, many writers, actors, poets, and artists who would not be welcome in other Arab lands are warmly appreciated in Lebanon.

The Lebanese have always had a great love and respect for literature. In the 18th century, the Lebanese rediscovered the stories and poems of ancient Arab writers and helped renew interest in them throughout the Arab world. Today, poets and novelists such as Georges Shehade and Michel Chiha are more popular with Lebanese.

The Castle of St. Gilles in Tripoli

Lebanon's most famous literary figure is poet, novelist, and artist Khalil Gibran. Born in the Lebanon Mountains in 1883, Gibran moved to Boston, Massachusetts, when he was a small boy. When he reached college age, he returned to Lebanon to attend a university in Beirut. He later went to Paris to study art. Although he is now recognized as a literary genius, Gibran first became known for his paintings and line drawings. When he began to write poetry, he sometimes illustrated his poems with his own artwork. Gibran was fluent in three languages, and wrote in Arabic, French, and English. Today, his works have been translated into dozens of languages. Although he remained a Lebanese citizen, Gibran spent most of his adult life in New York City. His literary works include *The Broken Wings*, *Mirrors of the Soul*, and *The Procession*, but he is known around the world for his masterpiece, *The Prophet*. Khalil Gibran died in 1931 at the age of 48.

Lebanon has 15 libraries, including the National Library in Beirut, where United Nations documents are stored. For most of the 20th century, the country's cultural life has centered around its universities, especially the prestigious American University of Beirut, which boasts an excellent library. In recent years, museums, research institutions, and art galleries have become the focus of cultural interest.

Music and Dance

Music plays an important part in the life of the Lebanese. They love to sing Lebanese folk songs, and at least one family member can usually play the *oud*, a pear-shaped instrument (similar to a

The Temple of Jupiter in Baalbek is more than 1,000 years old

lute) that is plucked with a quill. The men who make these ouds in suq shops will happily take a minute to plunk out a tune for a prospective buyer.

Folk music played on the oud accompanies the Lebanese national dance, the *dubke*. When the oud music begins, dubke dancers hold hands and form a line or a circle. Men, women, and children of all ages participate. The Lebanese usually dance the dubke at a *huflee* (dinner-dance). Lebanese communities in the United States and other foreign countries organize frequent huflees, where they can eat Lebanese food and dance to the music of the oud.

Ancient Ruins

After the Romans conquered Lebanon, they constructed many beautiful buildings there. The most famous Roman ruins are at

Baalbek, about 40 miles (65 kilometers) northeast of Beirut. The Romans used this location, named after the Canaanite god *Baal*, to build temples to their own deities, such as Jupiter, Bacchus, and Venus. Travelers today can still find these ruined temples in Baalbek, not much changed from the days when Romans living in Lebanon worshipped there.

In 1922, European archaeologists working in Baalbek took a break from their digging and began reciting poetry aloud. The acoustics of the setting made their words ring with such clarity that they decided to organize a performance. Every July and August since that summer day, famous acting companies from around the world have come to Baalbek to participate in plays and dances, just as the Romans did centuries ago. This is just one more way in which modern Lebanon maintains its links with its ancient past.

The Romans were also great road builders, and the marble paving stones from their highways still lie under weeds and underbrush. Because the Romans were fond of designing colorful mosaics into the road surfaces, archaeologists are often pleasantly surprised by colorful pictures as they dig.

At Tyre, a fortress city on the southern coast of Lebanon that the Phoenicians called "Queen of the Waters," archaeologists have discovered a Roman *necropolis* (burial ground). Strewn about the ruins are marble ornaments, urns, and an incredible collection of skulls and bones, grisly proof that here was the final resting place of the Romans—and later, the Crusaders—who had conquered the city.

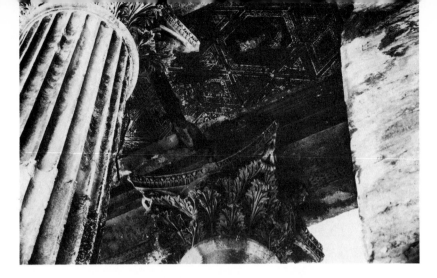

The ornate, carved ceiling of the Temple of Bacchus, god of wine

The oldest excavated ruin in Lebanon is the Biblical city of Zarephath, now called Sarepta. The Hebrew prophet Elijah visited the city and—according to the Old Testament—miraculously brought a Phoenician boy back to life. Discovered in 1970 under a wheat field, Zarephath is the only Phoenician city that was not built over by succeeding conquerors. It remains unchanged since before the time of Christ and gives detailed evidence of what life was like then. History surrounds the Lebanese, who accept the legacy of the ancient settlers as part of everyday life.

Like every nation, Lebanon has festive national holidays when work stops and everyone celebrates. The most important is Independence Day, November 22. Martyrs Day, in May, recalls the execution of Lebanese patriots by the Turks in 1916. Christians celebrate Christmas, New Year's, and Easter, and Muslims celebrate New Year's and *al-Adha,* the Prophet Muhammad's birthday.

85

Ancient Land in a Modern World

Lebanon has been at the center of world events since the brilliant Phoenicians lived along its shores more than 5,000 years ago. Our alphabet, the European chivalric tradition, and everyday conveniences such as glass mirrors and cosmetics all originated in Lebanon. One of the most important books in the history of western

The ancient and the modern exist side-by-side in Lebanon, as these two bridges attest

civilization—the Bible—takes its name from the Lebanese city of Byblos.

Lebanon's past is filled with events that have shaped world history. The troubles that plague the country today can be traced to many of these events: the Crusades, the abuses of the Ottoman Empire, the post-World War I French mandate, the partition of Palestine, and the subsequent wars between the Arab states and Israel.

Before the civil war began in 1975, Lebanon had managed to endure these problems and build a prosperous, relatively peaceful nation. Bankers and businessmen had made Lebanon a powerful force in the world economy, and travelers from Europe and the

As it has many times over the centuries, war has ravaged the ancient city of Beirut

Americas flocked to Lebanon to vacation at sophisticated resorts and to shop in the chic boutiques of Beirut. Today, vacationers avoid the war-torn nation, and much of Beirut lies in ruins.

Lebanon's civil problems did not develop overnight, and they will not be easily resolved. Political equality, economic stability, and a solution to the Palestinian refugee problem must be achieved before life in Lebanon can return to normal. Unfortunately, none of these problems can be solved while fighting in the streets and disorganization within the government continue.

Although Lebanon has faced invasion, repression, and bloodshed throughout its 5,000-year history, the country has endured. The Lebanese people know that of all the Great Empires of the Old Testament, theirs alone has survived to modern times. They have no intention of giving up now.